NUMBER 383

THE ENGLISH EXPERIENCE

ITS RECORD IN EARLY PRINTED BOOKS
PUBLISHED IN FACSIMILE

THE PROCEEDINGS OF THE GRISONS

n.p. 1619

DA CAPO PRESS
THEATRVM ORBIS TERRARVM LTD.
AMSTERDAM 1971 NEW YORK

The publishers acknowledge their gratitude
to the Curators of the Bodleian Library, Oxford
for their permission to reproduce
the Library's copy
(Shelfmark: 4°.E.2.Art BS (2))
Library of Congress Catalog Card Number:
78-171760

S.T.C. No. 12390
Collation: A-M4

Published in 1971 by
Theatrum Orbis Terrarum Ltd.,
O.Z. Voorburgwal 85, Amsterdam
&
Da Capo Press
- a division of Plenum Publishing Corporation -
227 West 17th Street, New York, 10011
Printed in the Netherlands

ISBN 90 221 0383 8

THE PROCEEDINGS OF THE GRISONS, IN THE YEERE 1618.

WHEREIN ARE TRVELY and cleerely laid open the lawfull and vrgent causes of calling an Assembly of the Commons: and of their due proceeding and Honourable prosecution of Iustice, which they were enforced to vse against some false and perfidious Patriots, in a full Congregation, and with absolute power met together at TOSANA.

IMPRINTED AND PVBLISHED BY Commandement of the Lords the Heads, the *Counsailours and Commons of the Three Confe*derations of the Renowned Free States of the *Grisons*: in maintenance of the Truth, and remoouing all manner of calumniation.

ANNO. 1619.

To The Reader.

H*Ee that will take an exact Suruey of the known World, beginning at home, and going as farre as Trauell & History can lead him, shall finde few people which are* Aboriginalls, *and first Inhabitants of the Cities or Countries they now possesse: But by settling of Collonies, or In-roads and Inundations of Warre, haue been transplanted. The* Saxons *hither: the* Cimbrians *into* France: *the* Gaules *into* Italy: *the* Vandalls *into* Spaine: *the* Greekes *into the Kingdome of* Naples: *the* Scythians *into* Turky: *the* Turks *into* Greece; *And these* Grisons *into this part of the* Alpes *anciently called* Rhetia, *then* Canninia; *after, the vpper* Slesia, *and now lastly, in their own Language* **Growpyndter** *or Cõfederations.*

This Countrey had the name of Rhetus, *who fled out of* Tuscany *from the fury of the* Gaules, *in the yeere* 187. *before the comming of Christ, and led with him many of the Inhabitants about* Florence, Pisa, *and* Lucca, *seating them in these high & in-accessible Mountaines: And as a few weather-beaten* Troians *laid the foundation of* Great Rome, *and some few fugitiue Citizens of* Vincenza, Padoa, *and other Townes in* Lombardy (*fleeing the rage of the barbarous* Gothes,) *planted themselues in the* Adriatick *Marishes, where they first began the re-*

nowned Venice: So this handfull of Tuſcans here planting and ſettling themſelues, are now growne to a warlike, ſtrong, and populous Nation. Such a fruitfull mother of children is Neceſſity, begotten by old Time their Father; that (as the mother of Cyrus dreamed) there ſprings a Vine in her wombe, by which in time whole Countries are ouer-ſhadowed.

This Countrey lyeth betweene the Degrees 46. and 44. in Latitude: part in Germany, and part in Italy; diuided by the Ridge of the Mountaine Splugen: On this ſide they ſpeake Dutch, on the other, Bergamaſque Italian. They haue free exerciſe of both Religions, Reformed and Romane. Here the Riuers of the Rhein and Teſin haue their heads; that, diuiding it ſelfe into ſeuerall Branches, and diſemboking into the German Ocean; this other falling into the Po, is carried by him into the Venetian Gulph. It confineth East vpon Tiroll, Weſt vpon the Swiſſe-Cantons, North vpon Conſtance, Friburg, and ſome parts of the Houſe of Auſtria, and South vpon the Countrey of Bergamo and State of Millan. The hither part is Mountainous, and therefore not ſo well able to ſuſtaine the Inhabitants; yet are there many fruitfull Valleys, which, (beſides their frugall and parſimonious maner of liuing) ſupply that want. Among theſe is Valtelina on the Italian ſide; for this is ſo plentifull of Corne, Cattle, Wines, & other fruits, as any part of Europe. The chiefe Townes of this fruitfull Valley, are, Bormio, Sondrio,

Tirano,

Tirano, Poſclauio, Morbegno, Traona, *and* Telo, *whereof the Valley takes the name, wherein are aboue* 100000. *ſoules. The part on this ſide hath many Caſtles and Townes, whereof* Coira *is the chiefe. It ſtandeth vpon the Riuer* Laſgar; *it embraced the Chriſtian faith the yeere* 448. *and in* 744. *had many priuiledges granted by* Charlemain, *and the Biſhop thereof made Rector of* Rhetia: *Among other Liberties it hath the coyning of Money, which paſſeth currant through the whole Country.*

The nature and manners of this people may bee read by the Character of the Swiſſes: *For, lying in the ſame Latitude, and inhabiting the like Mountaines, herein alſo they are like vnto them. A people giuen to Tillage and Planting their grounds; feeding vpon Butter, Cheeſe, Fiſh, Bread, Rootes, Wine, and but ſmall ſtore of Fleſh; vſing little Merchandize, but much manifacture, borne to Armes, and brought vp to labour; much addicted to exerciſe, eſpecially the Harquebuſe, hauing in diuers Townes and Villages Prizes for them which doe beſt. They are alſo much delighted with hunting in the Mountaines, of wilde Goates, Bucks, Beares, Wolues, and wilde Boares: holding it a great honour to take of theſe Beaſts, and for a Trophey to naile their heads on their gates; for which alſo ſometime the State rewards them. They are (onely on this ſide the Countrey) ſubiect to the Swiſſe and Dutch fault of exceſſiue drinking.*

Their Countrey is diuided into three Cantons or Con-

federations.

federations. The first is called,The Confederation of Cadè, *or* Ca-di-Dio:*(that is, Gods House:) the second is,* Lega Grisa : *and the third,* Lega delle Dritture, *or Iurisdictions.* Cadi Dio *containes the City & Territory of* Coira, *the Valley of vpper and lower* Agnadina, *with* Bregaglia: Lega Grisa *contains the Valley of* Mesolce, *and* Calanca, *with the Lands of* Rogoret *&* Musocco, *with other Valleys besides, on this side the Ridge of the Mountaines: the* Dritture *containe the rest of the Countrey. The first comprehendeth* 21. *Comminalties or Corporations : the second* 19. *the third* 10.

These three Cantons make the Confederation Generall: for though each of them haue their peculiar Magistrates, Lawes, Customes, and Iustice ciuill and criminall, yet the highest power and last Appeale is to the Senate or Assembly of the Three Cantons together : called by them the Pibach. *Whereunto the first Confederation sends* 23. *Deputies or Commissioners: the second* 28. *and the third* 14. *Where, they propound, consult, and determine onely that, for which they haue direction and command from their seuerall Cantons. To this Senate likewise belongeth to treat and conclude Peace or Warre, to make or reuoke Alliances and Leagues, to establish or abrogate Statutes and Lawes, to determine any difference betweene either of the Cantons, or resolue any businesse concerning the generall good of the whole Countrey. The places of Assembly are these;* Coira *in the first Confederation :* Illantum

tum *in the ſecond : and* Dauoſium *in the laſt. But if the Three Confederations are to treat a Buſineſſe, which they would haue kept ſecret , there are onely admitted into Councell, the Conſull of* Coira, *the Prouinciall Iudge of the* Lega Griſa, *and the Amano or chiefe Iuſtice of the* Dritture: *yet the voice to confirme all , is that of the* People; *if there be any Appeale. For controuerſies among themſelues thus : If a difference ariſe betweene the Three Confederations, three or foure perſons out of each are deputed (with diſcharge of their Oath to their owne Confederation) to arbitrate and compound the buſineſſe. If two be at difference, the third determines it. If between any of the Comminalties , the Senate of all Three Confederations ioyntly depute Iudges of the buſineße. If betweene a priuate man & the Confederations, two or three Iudges are appointed out of euery ſeuerall Confederation. If two Confederations haue a difference with the third, ſixe of the two Confederations, and ſixe of the third are choſen for Iudges : and in caſe theſe agree not, one onely Iudge is choſen by the voice of all the Commons.*

The firſt League was made betweene the Biſhop of Coira, *and the Prouinces about him, in the yeere* 1441. *The next betweene the Abbot of* Zizatis , *the Count of* Mauan, *and the Baron of* Bezuns, *with them of* Coira ; *this was called* Lega Griſa, *as that former* Lega Cadè: *after this, the Comminalties of* Segouia *made League with the two former, and was called* Lega delle Drit-

ture.

ture. *And lastly, in the yeere* 1470. *they all Colleagued together. But in the yeere* 1471. *hauing difference with their neighbours of* Tiroll, *they all entred League with seuen Cantons of the* Swisse. *And lastly, the whole thirteene Cantons of the* Swisse, *with these of the* Grison *Confederation, and the seuen Wards or Sokes of the* Valesians, *ioyned all in League with* St. Gallo: *which Citie was first founded and inhabited by one* Sengall *a Scottish-man, with other of his Countrey, and after grew to haue large Territories and Priuiledges. Thus all these Cantons* Grison *and* Swisse, *with the* Valesians *and them of* St. Gallo, *being a great, Warlike, and powerfull Body, stand in the gates of* Italy, *as firme as the Mountaines wherein they liue, against any forraine force whatsoeuer.*

A larger Relation might be made of this People and Countrey: But because a great head holds no Symmetry with a small Body, this little shall suffice to giue light to the ensuing Declaration.

THE PROCEEDING OF THE *GRISONS*. 1618.

AMONG the manifold benefits, and gracious fauours granted vs by God, the libertie of our Church and Commõ-wealth wherby we order & gouerne our owne affaires, is not the least: Because by the lawfull vse and sweet fruition thereof, our Soules & Honours, Bodies and Goods, are freely enioyed and safely preserued from all vexation and trouble. Hence is it, that *Libertie* like a most precious Iewell hath been euer much endeared and desired of all men.

We therefore the Inhabitants of the ancient and high *Rhetia*, now called by the name of the three *Grison Confederations generall*, hauing long enioyed the ſweet fruits and benefits of the bleſſings of God, and of his Almightie power, manifeſtly ſhewed in the reall fortitude and valour of our religious Anceſtors, who for many ages haue poſſeſſed and preſerued both theſe liberties: It hath ſeemed moſt meet and requiſite to vs, the Heads, Counſellors, and Commons of both the free Religions of theſe our Countries, publikely and priuately to hold the ſame liberty much indeared, and highly prized, and as much as in vs lyeth, to continue it among vs, and to our poſteritie.

We could well haue wiſhed that theſe our times had beene ſuch, as we might like our valiant forefathers, haue continued in the ancient poſſeſſion of our owne, without any trouble or moleſtatiō: But as al things of this world are ſubiect to declination and decay; ſo alſo this free State of ours is with time not a little weakened, and the danger thereof ſo much increaſed in theſe our dayes, as it had runne into manifeſt precipitation and ruine, had not God in his mercy ſtirred vp the zeale

of

of our faithfull and good Compatriots to tame and chastise the corrupters of our Gouernment, and withall to conserue and settle it in the former freedome.

We are therfore willing, for satisfaction of those that desire to know what hath passed, and are rather louers of the truth then calumnies, to giue them this full, substantiall, and true aduertisement and accompt of what hath passed, not onely in the weakening of our State, and impayring of our reputation, but also in the lawfull proceeding and iust punishing of those perfidious ones, for the reestablishment of our Gouernment, and reparation of those Breaches they had made vpon the libertie of our Countrey.

The forme of our Common-wealth is *Popular*, and the choosing and displacing of the supreme Magistrate, Officers, Iudges, and Commissioners in our free Countries and of our Subiects, standeth meerely in the power of our *People*, who haue absolute authoritie by pluralitie of voices, to establish and abrogate Lawes, Leagues, and Affiances with Princes and forraine States, to make Warre or Peace, and to order and gouerne all other businesses belonging to the higher and lower Magistrate.

All these Liberties and Priuiledges of ours, some priuate Persons through their great wealth and authoritie, with Pensions, Corruptions, Friendships, and Adherences, haue sought to appropriate vnto themselues, and assume into their owne hands, not once, but diuers times, and in seueral places, and Cominalties, according as they haue had occasion: wherein their practices haue preuailed so farre, as not onely our free Patriots and Subiects, but euen Princes & forrain States, whatsoeuer they desired in our Commonwealth, they were forced to seeke it at their onely hands: towards whom these men vsed all manner of treacheries, vnfaithfulness, fals-hood, deceit, tyrannie, lewd practices, and violences; and among many other their abuses, they haue brought our Countrey into dis-reputation and scandall with all Princes and forraine States, by vndertaking high matters, and making great promises for large summes of money, and after through their perfidious tergiuersation, haue falsely broken their faith, and wrought the multitude som-

times

times one way, ſomtimes another, of whoſe ſimplicitie they made their vſe, and deceitfully ruled and ledde them to all their purpoſes.

And albeit this wofull eſtate of our affairs lay couered and hid as vnder a cloud, yet both the wiſer ſort of men among vs, and the *Commons* alſo, made ſuch daily diſcouery of the badde effects thereof, as they all did much lament their miſerable eſtate, and would moſt willingly haue remedied ſo great a miſchiefe, by a preſent reformation & lawfull proceeding: but they found no poſſible meanes to effect that fruitfully, which they deſired ſo earneſtly, by reaſon of the great and many adherents of theſe wicked men, and the diffidence and iealouſie that the common people had of all men. Hereupon all the true-hearted and honeſt men of our Countrey, well ſeeing that our State could not long ſtand in theſe diſorders, and yet not knowing how to repaire or amend them, they haue ſent vp their ſighs & prayers to God, the true protector of the afflicted: who hath now at laſt heard their wofull complaint, and ſhewed them the way to recouer their deliuery.

And besides those many graue and prudent persons of the body Politike, discouering the miserable estate of our Affaires; our Church-men also haue both earnestly and incessantly, priuately and publiquely, called vpon the State for a Reformation, and without any respect or feare of the danger they might incurre, they ioyntly preferred a Bill of Complaint, in the publique Assembly held at *Tauas* in the month of August, 1617. laying open their grieuances before the Three Confederations generall, and the ordinary Magistrate, for these so great and so vnsupportable inconueniences: and after a long commemoration of the present disorders and dangers, they modestly and earnestly pressed for a speedy and necessary Reformation.

Whereupon, the Magistrates calling into consideration the importance of the businesse, and other waighty reasons, resolued to propound these grieuances to the Councellers & Communalties of the *People*, as to the supreme Magistrate, whom they ought and must obey: And accordingly in a Synode

node holden in April, 1618. by the Protestant Diuines, they drew a Bill (the same in substance with that former) to be offered to the Councellers and Comminalties ouer all their Churches, earnestly requiring and humbly beseeching, that a speedy course might be taken by the States Generall, for remedy of so great an inconuenience, by all the faire wayes and ordinary meanes possible, without tumult or disturbance of the State, for the recouery of their liberty Spirituall and Ciuill; and for their freeing from the treacherous Complots, and perfidious Treaties, which some of our men haue entertained with diuers Princes, and forraine States: yet so, as not to prouoke these men to indignation, despight, or wicked deliberations, but rather to carry the businesse with such temper and moderation, that as the faithfulnesse & integrity of our fore-fathers is honoured and magnified by vs, so ours to our posterity might be recommended. And though this our endeuour to a milde and quiet proceeding hath beene published and made knowne to the world; yet the chiefe heads of that corruption haue laboured
with

with all their might, to crosse our descignes, to turne all to smoake, and to continue in their former practices and violent insolencies: Hereupon they of the Clergie haue with more vehemency vrged and pressed in their Sermons for a generall reformation of the State; and that the people would make choyce of some honourable Persons of the Country, such as were vnpassionate, and free from any interest or engagement with other Princes or States; to whom they might lay open the notorious perfidie of some men tyrannising amongst them, as an insolency no longer to be endured, and the principall cause of hindering the intended Reformation.

Into this number, the Adherents and Clyents of these treacherous and malicious men, presently intruded, forcing themselues by all possible meanes, to hinder and make frustrate all the good effects by good men desired. Whereupon the people despairing to bring the businesse to any wished yssue by so small a number of persons deputed, and finding that these tyrannisers ouer the State could no wayes be ouer-topped, but by a greater number, they pro ceed (not by way of resistance and force) but by pluralitie of voices, and by exclusion of all sorts of corruptions and false insinuations.

To which purpose the fiue Comminalties of the lower *Agnadina* lying vnder the *Waltasna,* with those of *Munstertal,* met together in the end of *Iune* last, earnestly by their letters solliciting all the other Cōminalties and Deputies of the Three Confederations to do the like, and iointly to assist them as a people oppressed and afflicted, their ancient power and authority being wrested from them,and engrossed and vsurped by certaine priuate persons; their voices falsified, their Lawes changed, and their goods daily and vnduly taken from them, vnder pretext of Magistracie & Iustice; to the end the new Lawes might be abrogated, their ancient Countrey restored to the former libertie,the Treasures of Princes and States forraine might not bee seazed vpon by priuate persons, without the knowledge and consent of the People; as also that Princes might be no more abused and entertained with their false promises,and perfidious treachery, but that a lawfull and impartial Court of Iuſtice might be eſtabliſhed by the whole Countrey, for the puniſhment of theſe their tranſgreſſions formerly committed, & for the defence of all true-hearted and honeſt Compatriots.

Vpon theſe inſtant intreaties and admonitions, there ioined preſently with them certaine Comminalties of the Iuriſdictions, & of the *Cadè*, with Enſignes diſplayde, and a great number of men, namely, they of the higher *Agnadina, Pregello, Poſclauia, Firſtenau*, and *Berguno*, reſoluing to aſſiſt their neighbours in the reformation of the publike State, and eſtabliſhing a lawfull and vnpaſſionate Court of Iuſtice, againſt theſe traiterous Delinquents to their common country; ſo that this proceeding might ſtand with the good liking & approbation of the other Comminalties. While this is in Treatie, *Rodulphus Planta* chiefe head of the tyrannizing faction dwelling at *Zernes*, in the lower *Agnadina* vpon *Waltaſna*, (notwithſtanding the ſafe-conduct which the people granted to him and his Enſignes) by aduice and counſaile of his adherents, fortifies himſelfe with men and munition in his houſe,

houſe, and Tower anciently called *Wilden berg*, placing there in Garriſon and in the ſtreets of *Zernes* 600. of his men, all good ſouldiers, taking an oath of them to defend him, to keepe the paſſages, throwe downe the Bridges, and to make open and hoſtile warre againſt the Confederats and his neere neighbours. He hath alſo demanded militarie ſuccours from others, thereby to drawe a ciuill Warre vpon his owne Countrey: but they of *Cadè* comming to aſſaile his houſe, and hee doubting leſt his men might be forced to render vp the Place and him in it, as not being able to make head againſt ſo great a power of the Confederates, perceiuing alſo that his taking of armes in ſuch hoſtile manner had greatly incenſed them againſt him, one morning very early with ſome few of his truſtieſt followers he eſcaped and fledde.

Shortly after, the houſe was aſſaulted, and that which in the firſt furie was not ſpoiled and conſumed, was taken by Inuentory, and carefully preſerued. Meane while the other Comminalties of the Three Confederations deputed their chiefe officers in *Agnadina*, who in their Aſſembly reſolued to ſend them an Embaſſage of certaine graue perſons both Spirituall & Temporall, with offer to ioyne with them, to reforme the Right & Iuſtice in the whole State, ſo that they would lay downe armes and diſmiſſe thoſe troupes. But receiuing anſwere, that the power and Adherents of the offenders was ſo great, as that without more aſſiſtance it was vnpoſſible to effect what they had propoũded, they gaue them good acceptance, & all the Comminalties of the Countrey laid downe their Enſignes, & vnited themſelues vnto them. Firſt in *Coira*, and then in *Toſana*, a village in the *Griſon* Confederation; where, in the Common Councell for the reeſtabliſhing of our State and gouernment, they haue reuiued certaine ancient and laudable Prouinciall Lawes, and made other new, vpon occaſions of theſe late tranſgreſſions (but with all good temper and moderation) whereunto they alſo that ſtaide at home, haue giuen their free conſent: the ſubſtance whereof is as followeth.

That both the Religions, Reformed & Catholique, in all our Countreys and Iuriſdicti-

ons

ons ſhall haue their free exerciſe, and euery Countrey be iointly defended by all the reſt in the Religion it profeſſeth.

That in all our Countreys euery Confederation, Comminaltie, Iuriſdiction, Perſons priuate, Nobles, and common People, ſhall be maintained in their Priuiledges, Liberties, Cuſtomes, Honours, and goods, and ſhall be content in euery controuerſie and ſuite of Law with one indifferent and vnpaſſionate Iudgement.

That our ſubiects ſhall be gouerned with Equitie and Iuſtice, & not fall into the iawes of rauening Wolues, as heretofore diuers times hath hapned.

That the Exchequer of euery ſeueral Comminaltie be from henceforth more faithfully looked vnto then formerly, and that it be not permitted to priuate men, to embezell and exhauſt the Publike Treaſure.

That no priuate perſon preſume henceforward, to treat with Princes and forraine States in matters of publike affaire, without eſpeciall commandement, vnder paine of Death: but yet, that all Leagues and Intelligences formerly made by order of our

Law, ſhall be faithfully and really obſerued.

And that faithfull and good neighbourhood be kept with the borderers and confiners vpon all our States, &c. with other particularities more at large.

Hereupon was eſtabliſhed a Court of Iuſtice, conſiſting of moſt godly, religious, and vpright men, not Partialiſts nor engaged by oath or particular gifts to any Prince or States whatſoeuer. In which Court euery Confederation hath appointed two & twentie Iudges, nine Inquiſitors, two Informers, one Secretarie, and two Clarkes. And becauſe it hath hitherto alwaies appeared, that our people haue been kept in better awe and order by the authoritie of Spirituall men, it was thought fitte that nine of the Clergy ſhould be alwaies Aſſiſtants in the Court, except it be when Sentence is to bee giuen. All which Iudges are bound by ſolemne oath, to diſcouer ſuch, as contrarie to our Law would treate with them, and eſpecially to regard no corruptions, bribes, friendſhips, enmities, factions, adherences, & the like, which might turne them from doing right: but onely to ſet before their eyes the glory of

God,

God,the ſafetie of our Countrey,and the due adminiſtration of Iuſtice.

The People being therefore met together, diuers ſuſpected perſons were committed to priſon, and many other conſcious of their own guiltineſſe and perfidie, ſtole away and fledde the Countrey.

Among the Priſoners,the chiefe was *Iohn Battiſta de Prouoſti*,commonly called *Zambra*,dwelling in the vpper *Veſpranela Bregaglia*, who both by the confeſſion of ſome already executed,by the teſtimony of diuers others,& by his own hand-writing,vvas cõuicted to haue counſailed & helped with other his adherẽts, that Fort *Fuentes* ſhould be built vpon the confines of the *Griſons*, and that the foundation being laid, & the Three Confederations reſoluing by armes to hinder the worke,as a thing contrary to the accord made with *Millan* 1531. and to their liberties, & priuiledges,he ſtayed the people being now ready in armes,with his falſe and perfidious pretences ; and meane while wrote to the State of *Millan* to goe on with the worke, the enemie forces being diuerted that would haue hindred the proceeding.

That

That before and after this, he had many priuiledges for tranſportation from the State of *Millan*, and many notable ſummes of money, not onely for the cauſes aforeſaid, but alſo for perſwading the people to a Capitulation with *Millan*, as a thing profitable and neceſſarie, which notwithſtanding had turned to our great preiudice and danger, not conſidering that hee had receiued from an Embaſſadour of another Prince two hundred crowns by way of Donatiue, and ſeuenty foure of annuall penſion, with promiſe to diſſwade our people from the ſaid Capitulation, & to hinder it (albeit at other times) the ſaid *Zambra* and other perfidious perſons haue receiued great ſummes of money of diuers Princes, vpon promiſe to worke their ends, by our Countries preiudice, and after hath moſt ſhamefully deceiued them, and perfidiouſly broken both his word and faith giuen them.

But when as *Zambra* had obſtinately and impudently denied both his own hand-writing, the confeſſion of others, and the teſtimonie of diuers honourable Perſons, he was by the Court condemned to take the *Strappata*,

pata, and beeing onely pulled vp without weight, at his letting down, freely confessed all the circumstances aforesaid, and that *Rodulphus Planta*, with others now dead, had beene authours of the counsaile for the said Fort *Fuentes*, during the time of the assembly of the Confederates in *Tauas* 1603. to constraine our people by this meanes (as he said) to hasten the League with *Millan*, euen as themselues pleased, which league the said *Planta* hath laboured to bee concluded and confirmed. And moreouer, besides his many Liberties and Licences for transporting Commodities, hee receiued from *Millan* at one time foure hundred Hungars, with promise of a gold chaine if the practice went forwards, besides many goodly Donatiues for all his house: as also, that he wrote to the Marquis of *Como*, aduertising him, that the powerfull resistance of the Enemy (meaning those of our Confederates) was now diuerted, and therefore hee should not faile to finish the Fabrike of the said Fort. And lastly, that hee resolued to conclude the League betweene *Millan* and fiue Comminalties only, who were deceiued and abused by him (with falſe corruptions and many faire promiſes) although none of the reſt entertained or accepted it, not conſidering that our common Countrey is bound by continuall and interchangeable obligation, not to accept any into their League, without the knowledge and conſent of the Maior part of the Three Confederations; All this with other things hee hath confeſſed, which is needleſſe to remember.

Whereupon Sentence was pronounced againſt him by the Court, vpon the 22. of *Auguſt* laſt paſt, that according to the Lawes hee ſhould bee beheaded and quartered by the common hangman, as a notorious Traitour to his Countrey: And that all his goods ſhould be confiſcate to the common Exchequer of the Three Confederations; ſaue onely thoſe allotted for paiment of his debts, and his wiues portion. It was further adiudged, that his houſe ſhould be demoliſhed and razed downe to the ground, and in the place thereof two Pillars ſet vp, for a perpetuall memory and deteſtation of his fact. But after Sentence giuen, great ſuite was made for him both by the Clergy and Laity, that in respect of his yeeres beeing seuentie foure, and of his nine Children, and many Kinsfolke, he might onely be beheaded, leauing it free to the Companies of Souldiours and common people, whether to pull down his house or no.

Answerable to this, & much more guiltie were found the two Brothers, *Rodulphus*, & *Pompeius Planta*, who to drayne the wealth from our Countrey, and draw it into their owne hands, as also the chiefe Magistracie and gouernment therof, they haue by a copartcinory infeoffed themselues in the Lands, and intruded themselues into the Tutelage of all our great Widowes and Orphans. The Marriages of great persons were wholly at their disposing, by meanes wherof they procured great power and adherencie, ruling and commanding not onely the Subiects of *Valtelina*, but euen the Prouincials themselues, at their owne pleasure; nay, they tyrannously oppressed their own Confederates and free neighbours, violently entring vpon their Estates, vnder colour and pretext of Iustice, not sparing the liues of Laytie or Clergy, and receiuing large gifts of Princes and neighbour States, promising much, and performing little or nothing.

Vpon the 18. of *August* a Processe was framed against *Pompeius Planta* of *Zernes*, dwelling at *Paschale* in *Donlesch*, who long before the Sẽtence was fled his Country: for that it clearely appeared by his owne hand-writings, & by Letters of his Brother *Rodulphus*, and diuers witnesses, that the said *Pompeius* had vsurped vpon the libertie of his Country, & like a false Traitour had had secret practice with forraine Princes, by which the Commonwealth was brought into eminent losse, & imminent precipitation. Moreouer, that hee had vsurped the supreme Magistracie in his owne Lieutenancy of *Forstenau*, which hee procured of the Bishop of *Coira* for terme of thirtie yeeres, contrarie to the Law and custome of the Countrey, taking bonds of other Officers preferred by him to like places of Magistracie, not to vndertake or conclude any businesse of importance without his knowledge, or of his Brother. Hee hath vvith the money of forraine Princes, placed all such in the supreme gouernments of their common Countrey,

as

as ſtood affected and addicted to them, and of vvhom they might ſerue themſelues in all occurrences, at their owne will & pleaſure, as appeares (among others) in *Lucio da Monte*, to vvhom he gaue at one time two thouſand Florens of forraine Princes money, and helped him to diſtribute them, that by this meanes hee might the more eaſily obtaine the office of ſupreme Iudge Prouinciall of the *Griſon* Confederation, without disburſing one pennie of his owne, as by his Letter to the ſaid *Pompeius* appeareth: wherby he was forced to execute his office at the beck and command of *Pompeius*, that euery buſineſſe might vvholly depend vpon him, might paſſe after his humour, and bee done out of his head, and not according to the ancient Liberty of our Countrey.

He hath boldly coozened and abuſed ſuch Princes and forraine States as gaue him any truſt: For once he was Broker for *Monſieur Paſquale* the French Embaſſadour, to receiue & diſtribute ſix thouſand Crownes, to be employed, that the League wee had contracted vvith *Venice*, might bee renounced by vs, before the full date were expired.

In consideration whereof hee receiued a great present to his owne proper vse and behoofe, besides three hundred Crownes in Donatiue, and two hundred Frankes of annuall pension, vvhich he thought too little, as appeares by a Letter of one of his Adherents, bearing date 12 *July* 1612. Yet contrarily, hee vvrites to his Brother *Rodulphus*, and giues him Counsell to promise the State of *Venice*, that if they vvould grant him a Collonels place vvith 500. Crownes of yeerely pension, both in time of Warre and Peace, vvith some honourable presents besides, that then hee vvould secretly further their demaunds: and toward *France*, *Millan*, and *Austria*, he vvould seele vp one of his eyes, (such are the very expresse words of his Letter) vvherein he further signifies, that in case his brother vvere not satisfied with the command of a French company, and that their fallhood and double dealing were discouered, that then hee vvould fall from *France*, vnder colour of more vrgent reasons, the better to palliate his falshood, and excuse himselfe to neighbour Princes. In

which

which Letter also we find these very words; Monsieur Gueffier *the French Embassadour here resident, would willingly there were a diuision and sedition among vs, and that wee should earnestly labour* Maximilian Mora *the Millanese Secretarie, that they would refuse vs intercourse and commerce with them of that State: but I thinke he doth it to spare his Crownes, that we might be wholly at his deuotion, & bound to no body else: as though that passage were only in the power of the French.*

In another of his to his Brother, bearing date the 15. of *April* 1616. hee writes thus: That cōcerning the Leauy of Souldiers here by the *Venetians*, he meant to giue his cōsent and assistance; but with condition, that *Signor Padauino* should performe what hee had promised, (that is, large Donatiues) and though his Brother held still his *French* Cōpany, yet he would doe his vttermost for the *Venetians* without any danger; writing also in these vvords: *They cannot so easily fall vpon vs, we haue (God be praised) more Souldiours strangers then they: as for the French, I esteeme them lesse and also worse, for they cannot so easily piece their businesse with the* Vene-

tians,

tians,*and these men euer grow vpon vs. Lord God! who knowes what will become of the businesse? We must put it to the venture: and yet for conclusion, I am fully resolued in spite of the* French, *to act somewhat for mine owne best aduantage.* Moreouer, in the said Letter wee finde these words: *I haue been ill at ease these two daies, else had I aduised the* French-man, *vpon whom I will haue an eye that hee shall not betray vs; we shall not need many words, but doe that which is requisite.* And yet the better to hide his secret practices, he hath written to the neighbor Princes, suggesting vnto them the meanes (as appeares by his Letter) how they might hinder the League the *Venetians* demanded of vs in time of their Warres, that it might take no effect: and albeit hee hath euer made faire shewe to the *Venetian* Commonwealth, yet hee hath wrought our people with mony and other meanes, to stop their passage through our Country, to ioyne in League with the *Millanese*, and to make him absolute Master of all our passages, according to the intolerable Articles of the League propounded to vs by *Millan*.

Hee bound himselfe by strict Oath to the

Arch-

Arch-Dukes Highnesse of *Insprush*, vpon receiuing a great Lordship to be held in Fee of him, as appeares by that Princes Letters of the 29. of *Nouember* 1613. the 26. of *Ianuary* 1615. and the 15. of *October* 1615. to be alwaies faithfull to his Highnesse as his Councellor and Vassall, and to supply him with Souldiours at his demaund, against all his enemies, wheresoeuer, howsoeuer, and whensoeuer he should haue occasion. And yet on the other side hee greatly mis-prized and vilified the authoritie of that Prince in a Letter of his to his Brother *Rodulphus*, bearing date the 15. of *April* 1616. and counsailed him against Iustice and the Prerogatiue of that Prince in *Agnadina*, but withall, that the businesse might be cautelously and cunningly carried.

Afterwards hee solemnely protested by Oath in the publike Assẽbly at *Tauas* 1617. that he was not (effectiuely) bound to any forraine Prince or State: and yet without regard of his Oath, wherby as a person now placed in Authoritie he stood bound, nor hauing respect to his own Honour, or reputation of our common Countrey, he discouered to his Highnesse whatsoeuer was concluded in our Councell, suggesting to that Prince, that he should terrifie vs with threats, in case wee vndertooke the Treatie of a League with *Venice*; and protesting, that if we receiued any hurt thereby, the blame should lye vpon none but our selues, as appeares by the Contents of his Letter dated the 10. of *May* 1615. and of his answer from *Inspruch* the 25. of the same moneth.

He perswaded also his Highnesse, that he would earnestly sollicite the Three Confederations Generall, both by Letter and other meanes, that the Inhabitants of *Tauas* who haue many priuiledges, might become his Subiects; as appeares by his Letter of the 7. of *August* 1614. Hee braggeth in another of his to his Brother, that hee had intercepted some Letters of forrain Princes addressed to the Confederations Generall: and because his practices succeeded oft-times to his wish, his Brother and he vainely thought themselues so powerfull, as they might doe what they list in their Countrey: the reason was, for that in all occasions of conuenting the Three Confederations Generall together, they

they ſtil ouerſwayed the Councels & Iudgements vvith their pluralitie of voices, great Clientele, and Adherence, &c. But as the children of darkneſſe are wiſe in their generation, ſo theſe Brothers had prouidently complotted, that in caſe their perfidious treacheries were diſcouered, they would then retyre themſelues into *Valtelina*, where their chiefeſt friends and dependants were, or elſe ſome other-where to fortifie and arme themſelues, and ſo make a Ciuill warre vpon their natiue Countrey, as *Pompeius* had formerly threatened: who beeing aduertiſed that the Clergy would oppoſe his deſſeignes, (and eſpecially the *Spaniſh* League he intended) he audaciouſly anſwered amongſt other his inſolent ſpeeches, *Let them looke to themſelues, leſt they runne the like fortune that* Zuinglius *did in the warre of* Zurich.

Hee therefore hauing committed theſe and many other heinous crimes, and hauing brought his Countrey into great troubles in it ſelfe, and great diſ-reputation and diſgrace with other Princes, through his temerarious perfidie; after many Citations by forme of Iuſtice and Law, hee was vpon his contumacie banished for life frō the Three Confederations Generall, with a Fine and Donatiue of a thousand Crownes to him that should bring him aliue into the hands of Iustice; and fiue hundred Crownes out of the publike Treasurie to him that should bring in his head. And in case he were taken in any of our Countreys or Iurisdictions, that without further Processe hee should be executed by the common Hangman, & his quarters to be set vp vpon the high vvayes; his house to be razed, and two Pillars of infamy set vp in the place; his goods confiscate to the Exchequer of the Three Confederations Generall, and no man vpon paine of death euer to speake or treat for his Pardon: whosoeuer should lodge him, to forfeit a thousand Crownes, and to be banished (as he is) for life: and if any of our Comminalties should harbour him, to bee excluded (as perfidious) out of the Letters Patents of the Confederation.

Vpon the 26. of *August*, another Processe was framed against *Rodulphus Planta* of *Zernes*, Captaine of the Prouince of *Valtelina*, and criminall Iudge in *Zernes* aforesaid and

the

the neighbour Comminalties ; Captaine likewise of a Band of the Confederates for the French Kings seruice. Against this man it was prooued by seuerall Processes, Confessions, Testimonies, Writings, and memorials of his own and his Brothers, as also by Letters of other his Adherents, that hee had by many and strange practices brought the whole power of the Supreme Magistrate of the Three Confederations into his owne hands, vsing it with much tyrannie against both publique and priuate persons, and falsely practising as well against our own Countreymen, as against Princes and forraine States: He hath treacherously betrayed his Countrey through his perfidious auarice, as also all others that trusted him; bringing vs all into discredit and displeasure with other States, and thereby hath beene the cause of many Deliberations most preiudiciall and pernicious vnto vs.

He hath intruded into the Magistrats place and power after this manner: His Highnes of *Inspruch* hath some priuiledge in choosing the criminall Iudge of the lower *Agnadina* euery S^t. *Georges* day, with the will and consent of the common people. By this meanes and that Princes fauour, *Planta* hath beene chosen Iudge diuers yeeres together: which time being expired, hee hath sought no renewing or confirmation by the whole Bench of Iustice, but hath boldly vsurped the power, as if it had beene his owne by inheritance or purchase: Moreouer, of his own meere Authoritie hee hath arrogated the decision of ciuill or criminall causes, by choosing those for Iudges that were for his purpose, and he that would not be pliable to his will, and submit himselfe to his Tyrannie, was instantly cassed, and another more obedient to his pleasure chosen: whereby hee hath brought the Supreme power of the Magistrate to be at his deuotion and disposition without any contradiction, in all places as farre as their whole Iurisdiction extendeth.

He hath also preferred others to places of gouernment, especially such as could aduance any Creature and Adherent of his to the Supreme Magistracie, but yet with condition, that neither he nor they should conclude any thing of importance, without his

aduice

aduice and counsaile ; but should carry the businesse by his direction onely, against the libertie of our common Country. According to which complot he hath taken into his protection in his Castle of *Coira*, *Iohn* Bishop of that place, before he had obtained his Libertie or Pardon : a man who for his treacherie to his Countrey and other offences, had been banished from the Three Confederations Generall, by a lawfull and vnpassionate iudgement of both the Religions : which the said *Planta* hath done, to haue the Bishop euer ready at his will and command for the appointing of any Officers (chiefly within the precincts of *Cadè* :) In consideration whereof, the said Bishop granted to *Pompeius Planta* the Lieutenancy of *Forstenau* for thirtie yeeres : where, as chiefe in the Bishops name, hee hath power to appoint three Burgomasters ; and so hath he dealt with the yong Lord of *Rasiuz*, and many other.

He hath also obtained of diuers great Families, that when they shall haue any suites in Law depending in their Comminalties, hee onely may haue the decision of their con-

controuersies, gaining power by that means to establish in the Office that man whom he shall preferre: and these few yeeres last past, some Gentlemen of good qualitie in the vpper *Agnadina*, desirous to enioy their Liberties and custome of free Election, he vvith his false and wicked practices so handled the matter, as none but his owne Dependents were chosen to any Offices: and seeking in the disposition of other Charges also, to infringe the strength of pluralitie of voices, he hath beene the cause of sixe mens death, besides the endangering of many Iudges liues by force of Armes.

And knowing that *Monsieur Pasquale* was at that time in great credit and power with vs, he secretly contracted with him, as appeares by a Letter of his Brother, and another of one of his Adherents, bearing date the 22. of *February* 1611. and the 11. of *Ianuary* 1612. and by a Letter of *Monsieur Pasquales* owne hand: vvhich Letter stood *Planta* in good steade, and serued fitly his purpose; for hauing got strict Intelligence vvith the Embassadour, euery one that desired a Pension, vvas forced to receiue it

through

through *Planta's* hands; by vvhich meanes he got of the Embassadour large summes of money, new pensions, and augmentation of the old, as shall more amply be related in the summing vp of his practices.

Moreouer, he hath much increased his Authoritie by meanes of Marriages; for being in great reputation and power with his kindred and Adherents, they ranne all to him in businesse of greatest importance: & if they bound themselues to stand wholly to his direction, they got what they desired, else not.

He hath alwaies kept Spies and Informers both at home and abroad, to vnderstand the deliberations of those hee suspected: and finding them vpon information contrarie to his deseignes, hee vvould first seeke to winne them; if not, he would prosecute and pursue them to their vttermost ruine. And to make himselfe yet more powerful, he would falsifie and corrupt the Statutes and Lawes of the Countrey within his Iurisdiction, enlarging or restraining them to his best aduantage.

With these and the like sleights these

thirtie fiue yeeres together, hee is growne ſo great, as for a long time hee hath engroſſed into his hands all the important buſineſſe of our Subiects, whom hee hath bound to him by diuers preſents and bribes, to elect his creatures & Dependents into the Offices of ſeuerall Comminalties: by whom hee might after ſerue his owne turne to infringe the Lawes, to ſtirre vp tumults againſt honeſt men, and to gouerne all at his owne pleaſure; vſing this his power with much tyrannie againſt all ſorts of people both Spirituall and Temporall.

Hee hath moſt inſolently vſurped vpon the Iuriſdictions of the Comminalties, depriuing them of their Liberties, and forcing them to depend wholly at his deuotion in the choiſe of their Magiſtrates, not daring to ſpeake or aduiſe any thing againſt him, for feare of loſing his fauour; but they all ranne as he would haue them.

He hath too rigorouſly condemned poore men of the Countrey for very ſmall faults, and then compounded with them for no ſmall gifts and bribes, without the knowledge or conſent of the Court: whereunto the poore men were enforced to auoid his tyrannous perſecution, and were bound by Oath not to complaine or once ſpeake of the wrong he had done them: whereof we haue here ſet downe ſome few particulars among many hundreds; and theſe they be:

A man beeing fledde vpon a certaine cryme committed, and dead in the Mountaines; *Planta* forceth the poore heyres of the dead man to pay two hundred and ſixtie Florens for his eſcape: contrary to the Lawes of the Countrey, which condemne a man only in ten Florens for his flight: which Fine is alſo to be payed to the whole Court, not to the criminall Iudge alone.

If at any time an offender endited and conuicted, had accuſed another of ſome ſmall crime, he would not diſcouer the euidence, nor call the partie in queſtion, till after the execution of the Accuſer: And though the partie accuſed knew not whether he vvere indeed charged by that other, or that it vvas a thing of *Planta's* owne forging, and much complained that hee vvas not called to his anſwere vvhile the Accuſer liued: yet was hee forced to compound vvith him for round ſummes of Money, to auoid his indignation, and vniuſt perſecution.

Two men confeſſed vpon the Torture, that they had ſtolne a certaine quantitie of Wheate from a neighbour of theirs : the man hearing of their confeſſion, ſaid hee knew of none he had loſt : for vvhich word alone, *Planta* fined him ſecretly at fortie Crownes, threatning, that if he paid not the money, he would caſt him in priſon, and put him to Torture, to confeſſe whether he loſt any wheate or no

Vpon a time he ſending his Warrant for one accuſed, to appeare before him at *Zernes*, he demanded a horſe of a woman for that ſeruice, to ſend him backe to priſon, whoſe Husband vvas gone to the wood with him : *Planta* ſeemes offended that the horſe could not bee had : the poore Wife ſends preſently to her Husband, to make vvhat haſte he could with his Horſe from the wood : the good-man, though he came home preſently after the Iudge and the priſoner vvere departed, and made haſte after them to offer them his Horſe, he had anſwer,

that

that now they had got another to ſerue their turne: all this notwithſtanding, *Planta* fined the poore man in fiue and twentie Crownes, becauſe hee had not offered his Horſe before he went to the wood.

Two men being in ſuite for a matter not aboue halfe a Crowne, one gaue in euidence: *Planta* preſently laid to his charge that he had giuen falſe vvitneſſe; threatning him the Torture, and that he would plucke out his tongue by the rootes. Hereat the poore man was ſo much affrighted, as hee promiſed *Planta* a ſecret Donatiue of two hundred Crownes to bee leauied vpon his Lands, and was afterward forced to diſengage them of that morgage with a hundred and twenty Hungars, beſides threeſcore Crownes Fine for the accuſation, and fifty more for charges of the Court.

Foure free men of the Confederation, bringing from *Chiauenna* into *Finſcouia* ſome loades of Rice vpon their own horſes, and paſſing through the lower *Agnadina*, bartring their Rice for Wheat, they returned with their ſaid loading and Merchandize through *Zernes* : *Planta* preſently charged them by his cruell practice to make their market, and vent their commoditie in the vpper *Agnadina*, or elſe they ſhould bee fined for vſing their owne horſes, and not thoſe of his neighbours : who refuſing to ſatisfie him herein, they were fined at a hundred Florens.

One ſaid to a neighbour of his, that if hee had paid *Planta* the money hee ought him, he would not owe him the putting off of his cap : he was for theſe words onely, fined in an hundred Crownes.

He plotted that ſtrange ſtratageme in the vpper *Agnadina*, where he incenſed two germane brothers one againſt the other : and that ſide which hee abbetted hauing the vvorſe, he ſent to his aide two hundred and fiftie men ; to obtaine that by vnlawfull waies and open violence, which hee could not compaſſe by corruptions, promiſes, and menaces : By which tumult hee was the occaſion of ſix honourable mens death, beſides many other ſore wounded.

Hee hath alſo beene an Aſſaſſinate and bloud-ſucker of the Clergie : for a Prieſt of *Monſtertall* ſeeing his perfidious practices,

and

and ſpeaking ſomewhat freely of them, hee ſo perſecuted the man vvith his calumniations, as at length he cauſed him to dye by the hand of Iuſtice.

Likewiſe, they of the reformed Clergie oppoſing the Capitulations of the League propounded betweene our Confederations and the houſe of *Millan*, in the yeere 1617. and publiquely reprouing diuers other diſorders, ſome of them hee perſecuted vvith his criminall Authoritie; others he laboured to remooue from their Miniſterie; ſome hee violently ſet vpon in his owne perſon; ſome he impriſoned and threatned to doe worſe vnto them; vpon others his ſeruants bent their Piſtols, and Harquebuſies charged, menacing to kill them: Hee hath fined diuers men for ſpeaking well of their Doctors and Miniſters. Finally, the perfidie and falſhood of his notorious practices is vnſpeakeable: for many times hee takes bribes to the ſumme of a thouſand Florens and more betweene both parties in difference, and in the end ſhamefully deceiues the one and the other.

To defend a Traitour and ſaue him harme-

harmelesse from danger of the Law, hee tooke a bribe of a thousand and fiue hundred Crownes. In another case of difference, he tooke seuen hundred & eightie Crownes of one partie, and a thousand of the other, and then failed them both. In a difference of suite depending betweene two Comminalties, hee tooke foure hundred Crownes apiece, and effected nothing for either.

His treacherous practices against his Countrey cannot sufficiently be related, as appeareth by vvhat hath beene said, and by his indeuours at all times to make himselfe Lord of the Gouernment: as likewise appeareth by the Processe of *Zambra*, and other actions of his owne, vvhich tended to fauour and further the treacherous capitulation vvith the house of *Millan*, to depriue vs of our Priuiledges and Iurisdictions, and to enthrall vs vnder the power of forraine Princes. Among other meanes he hath vsed, hee hath also serued his turne of these which follow:

The yeare 1603. he complotted with *Iohn Battista Zambra*, to further or rather enforce a League aboue and against all other intelli-

gences

gences and Leagues wee had formerly contracted, labouring that the Fort *Fuentes* might be built, and withholding our people from hindring the proceeding of the said vvorke. And the Three Confederations Generall in the yeere 1606. being truely enformed that all their secrets of State vvere discouered to forraine Princes, they established a Priuy Councell of fifteene men, to the intent that all their Deliberations might bee entrusted to secret Confidence: whereupon *Planta* and his Complices being so debarred from the knowledge of any thing, raised that dangerous tumult in the yeere 1607.

Iohn-Peter Mera da Piur, hath also confessed *Planta's* Treason touching the Fort, and that he was moued by him and wonne by his subtill sleights, corruptions, and Donatiues, to the calling back of his forces, as by *Planta's* Letter to his Brother *Pompeius* appeareth, and by Letters of other his Adherents dated the 3. of *October* 1604.

In the yeere 1610. to our great losse and griefe, the French King *Henry* the fourth was murthered, after whose death, *Monsieur Pasquale* the French Embassadour resident with vs, ſent a ſecret diſpatch to *Millan* in the yeere 1611. to treat with *Signor Alphonſo Caſale*, Embaſſadour in *Switzerland* for the King of *Spain*, that he would cauſe a League or new intelligence to be made between the State of *Millan*, and the Three Confederations Generall: and to the intent the ſaid Treatie might not bee hindred, the ſaid *French* Embaſſadour and Captaine *Planta* beeing both agreed vpon the buſineſſe (though the *French* Kings were alwaies againſt it) hee gaue *Planta* ſixe thouſand Crownes of gold, and two thouſand and fiue hundred Frankes of yeerely penſion, to be diſtributed as he thought good, without being bound to make any account, that hee and his Adherents would help to breake the League with *Venice*, which was contrarie to the Treatie betweene *Millan* and vs: as appeares by the Letters of *Pompeius* and his Adherents in the yeere 1612. and by a Memoriall written with Captaine *Planta's* own hand.

The renunciation of the League between the State of *Venice* and vs beeing procured and bought by money, *Planta* preſently

drawes

drawes out some Articles of the League of *Zuz*: Wherein some Comminalties dwelling vpon the Passages, are bound not to grant passage to any whatsoeuer through our Countries, that all friendship and aide of ours towards the *Venetians* might be broken. And the said *Casale* hauing in the yeere 1617. required a League with vs, and free passage, in name of the house of *Millan*, they which were authors of the League of *Zuz*, and of the deniall of passage to the Souldiers of forraine States, were the first that granted the King of *Spaine* free passage for his Forces, through all our Countreys and vpon all occasions, contrary to what they had formerly concluded: So that the falshood of *Planta* and his Adherents doubly appeared.

Against these Treaties of *Planta* and other his Complices, diuers good Patriots both of the Clergie and Laitie so earnestly laboured, as they were by no meanes accepted: herevpon *Planta* much enraged, thought vpon a speedy and liuely reuenge, beginning to prosecute those of most honestie and reputation, farre more then formerly hee had done, and ſtirring them of the vpper *Agnadina* to tumult, hee made them riſe in Armes with Enſignes diſplayed, to thruſt violently *Signor Padauino* out of our Countrey, vvho had retyred himſelfe before their comming: he hath alſo conuented the people together, brought thither by his Adherents and Seruants, framing diuers barbarous Articles, and conſtraining all men to obſerue them.

The ſecond of which Articles was this: That no Church-man of any Comminaltie ſhould dare to ſpeake or giue his voice in any buſineſſe concerning the Countrey: though this be lawfull to euery free man of our State, be he neuer ſo poore and baſe: and this he did, becauſe in all his machinations and plots, hee neuer found ſtiffer reſiſtance then from the Clergie. Moreouer, they haue had diuers and ſundry conſultations vvith *Maximilian Mora* to put them to ſilence, and ſtop their mouthes altogether: and laſtly, they haue found it fit to forbid them by a generall Law, not to meddle with matters of State, or the good of their common Countrey, or to bee informers of the preſent corruptions. So much the Diuell

uell hath blinded their eyes, that they nei-ther can, nor vvill see or suffer the whole-some admonition of faithfull Subiects.

They haue also settled a Court of Iustice, the decrees whereof (by confession of some of the Iudges themselues) were wholly ma-naged and dispatched by the aduice and in-formation of the two Brothers onely. Iud-ges also were chosen, such as stood partially affected to forraine Princes, of whose libe-ralitie they had bountifully tasted: who al-so were bound by Oath to defend the Bi-shop of *Coira*, against our Prouinciall lawes, to which they were sworne: vvhich they did by many indirect waies, and by the pro-curement of the inwardest friends to the *Planta's*, who by their bad proceedings haue deceiued many honest men, and di-uers honourable Comminalties, with their large summes of money.

More especially, they haue persecuted the said Clergie, calling them to appeare before them, and charging them not to meddle, or once speake in the *Spanish* businesse, fi-ning some of them in grosse summes for ha-uing spoken too much: and among the rest,

 they

they brought one Preacher by force from his houſe in *Coira*, without any cauſe but meere malice; threatening impriſonment, and death, or baniſhment to others.

On the other ſide, they haue offered to maintaine the Biſhop of *Coira* with ſtrong hand: who (as is aforeſaid) had beene baniſhed by Proclamation out of the Three Confederations Generall, and hath lately beene charged by forme of Law with many notorious crimes: and not regarding his manifold tranſgreſſions, they haue conſented to his eſcape out of the Countrey, and granted free paſſage for his goods after him.

Theſe tumults *Planta* hath not onely cauſed, as is manifeſt by many vvitneſſes *Viua voce*, but he hath alſo granted tranſportation of Commodities, without knowledge of the State, in a time when the paſſages were ſhut, and commerce forbidden betweene vs and *Millan*: though at the ſame time his Brother *Pompeius* wrote to him, that *Monſieur Gueffier* the *French* Embaſſadour had importuned *Maximilian Mora*, to deſire the ſtopping of the paſſage and enter-course, alledging, that he desired a commotion and sedition among vs.

And now this present yeere 1618. some of our Comminalties rising in Armes to remedy this mischiefe, hee presently bound by Oath the men of his Circuit to demand aide of others, thereby to mooue a Ciuill warre, that the common people butchering one another, he might subdue the stronger part remaining, and so make himselfe vniuersall and absolute Lord of all the Countrey. But foreseeing that this plot vvould faile him, and doubting that hee should be cited to answere the Law for his notorious mis-demeanours, he presently fled: vpon his flight, he was according to custome diuers times summoned, and neuer appeared. Seeing therefore he hath vsurped the chiefe Authoritie of our Countrey, as to giue and abolish Lawes, to make and renounce Leagues, to create and depose Magistrates, to dispose of Warre and Peace, and hath vsed this his power with all manner of perfidie, deceit, violence, tyrannie, and Treason; he hath beene by the Law and Iustice of our Countrey, condemned to perpetuall banish-

banishment from all the Three Confederations Generall, and left free to the Birds of the ayre: with a reward and Fee of a thousand Crownes to him shall bring him aliue into our Countrey; and to him shall bring in his head fiue hundred Crownes; besides his freeing from the Proclamation, if hee stand banished for any other offence, but Treason against the State, or wilfull murther: which money shall be paid out of the Common Treasury: And in case he be apprehended in our Country, or yeeld himselfe into the hands of the Three Confederations Generall, that then the Magistrate shall call a Court of Iustice of the Three Confederations, and without any farther Processe shall order, that he be forthwith executed and quartered by the common Hangman, and his quarters to be set vp in the common high waies: all his goods to be confiscate to the Chamber of the common Treasurie, sauing the dowrie of his wife, and the paiment of his cleere debts; his house to be razed, and two pillars set vp in the place, to his perpetuall infamy: and that Comminaltie which shall refuse to execute this Sentence, and

shall

ſhall ſuccour him with meate, drinke or lodging, ſhall forfeit their Right in the Confederation, and beſides, for euery ſuch offence ſhall be fined in a thouſand Crownes: and if he be a priuate perſon, he ſhall be depriued of his honours, and forfeit a thouſand Crownes: but he that is not worth ſo much in goods or lands, ſhall forfeit his life: and laſtly, if any ſpeake of his Pardon, write to him, or talke with him, or ſhall receiue or reade his Letters, ſhall likewiſe loſe his life.

In this *Interim*, vpon the 22. of *Auguſt*, *Nicolo Ruſca da Lugano*, Arch-prieſt of *Sondrio* in *Valtelina*, was accuſed, who formerly had beene impriſoned by the People, for hauing conſpired with *Iohn-Paolo Quadrio* of *Ponte*, & *Vincẽzo Gatto* of *Coira*, to kil *Signor Scipione Calandrino* late Preacher in *Sondrio*, in caſe they could finde him vpon the State of *Millan*, or elſe to carry him out of our State, to *Millan* or to *Rome*, as diuers times heretofore it had happened to others; as *Michael Ciappino* hath publiquely confeſſed, both vpon the Torture and after: who being reſolued to act this his bloudy purpoſe, *Calan-*

drino had notice by ſome of his friends, that the Arch-prieſt lay in waite for his life, and had his Spies vpon him: as appeared by a Briefe of his ſent to *Ciappino* by a yong Lad; wherin he giues him aduertiſement, when, and in what place he might come with his complices, and in what manner hee might performe that felonious act: wherevpon *Ciappino* was impriſoned in the yeere 1698. in the moneth of *September*, vnder the charge of Captaine *Iohn Corn* of *Caſtelmur*: where, vpon proofe of the Euidence, hee ſuffered death, as appeares by his Proceſſe and the confeſſions vnder the hand and ſeale of the ſaid *Signor Capitano*. *Ciappino* had to this purpoſe made choiſe of certaine Ferry-men, *Andrea Serem da Como, Iohn Piſer da Traona,* and *Battiſta Domini da Menas,* who in the yeere 1594. *Iuly*, were all executed, becauſe being at the Ferry-place of the Riuer *Adda*, where *Calandrino* was retyred, they would violently haue haled him into their Barque; but they were apprehended by *Signor Capitano Artman de Artmani*, and the whole buſineſſe being proued againſt them, they were for the ſaid murtherous conſpiracie and

trea-

treaſonable plot condemned to die.

Moreouer, this *Ruſca* had ſhewed himſelfe a Rebel and diſobedient to the ſupreme Magiſtrate of the Three Confederations Generall, becauſe hee embezeled and defaced the Decrees and Records of that Office: and afterwards holding his Congregation in the Cloiſters at *Sondrio*, there were heard many ſeditious and rebellious words by diuers honeſt men in the ſtreets, which they haue fully teſtified and proued, and as ſince hath beene confirmed by *Nicolo Carbonera*, both vpon and after Torture: affirming moreouer, that hee had giuen counſaile to cancell ſome Decrees of his owne State, by the procurement of the *French* Embaſſadours, in whom *Signor Iulio della Torre* had great intereſt to preuaile, as a faithfull and truſtie friend of theirs: That he had alſo hindred the free courſe of preaching the Goſpell.

He had ſo farre made himſelfe Maſter of the peoples will, that the Officers of *Valtelina* fearing ſome ſodaine tumult & inſurrection, durſt not lay open his horrible crimes and tranſgreſſions. In the time while Fort

Fuentes was building, he retyred to *Morbegno*, where, (as is prooued by diuers Testimonies & his own confession) he perswaded the people, not to make warre with so Catholique a Prince as the King of *Spaine*, but to keepe their consciences free, and to aske him pardon for their fault: resisting by that meanes the Proueditor of the Confederations Generall, who was forced patiently to dissemble this rebellious affront: and albeit he was resolued to charge him herewithall before the Councellors and Comminalties, yet he deferred it till the fourth of *August* 1608. at what time hee was summoned before the Comminalties, and in *Nouember* after, before the Iustice Court of the Three Confederations Generall of both the Religions; but being conscious of his own guiltinesse, he neuer appeared.

He hath also by assistance of his Complices laboured to corrupt and drawe many men to his partie, as appeares by Letters of his written to a friend the 22, 23, and 24. of *December* the same yeere, as also by the testimonie of diuers honest men; wherevpon euen they that were corrupted by him, haue

receiued

receiued condigne puniſhment,bu
clemencie.

He hath held particular correſ
and ſecret conference with the C
ners of forraine Princes, and eſpe
hath had ſtrict intelligence an
with the diſloyall Rebels of our
fauouring many of their pernic
ſeignes, as appeares by writings o
and others: nay, during the time
fuſing paſſage and commerce wit
of *Millan*, he made a iourney tw
Citie, not without our great ſuſp
iealouſie. Which ſaid accuſatio
ming before the Court of Iuſtice,
Iudges calling into ſerious conſ
our ancient Lawes and proceedin
carefully peruſing and examining
ſaid Letters, as alſo thoſe written by
Sulmona Prieſt, the 6. of *Nouember* 1
Signor Philippe Biſhop of *Como* th
March 1610. and by Fryer *Francis*
ciall of his order in *Millan*, bearing
12. of *Ianuary* 1611. and by ma
Letters addreſſed to him, and by
monie of honeſt men heard and ap

they all appeare to the Court to be true and iuſtifiable.

This man notwithſtanding gaineſayed all, denied the confeſſions of thoſe had beene tortured and executed, made a ridiculous ſcoffe of the Letters and atteſtations, labouring to excuſe himſelfe and put off the matter with a ieſt: but withall he beſought the Court they would proceede no farther againſt him, but either ſend him to perpetuall baniſhment, or condemne him to the Gallies. Herevpon they adiudged him to bee tortured: the firſt day hee was hoiſed thrice without any weight; nor would hee confeſſe any thing: the ſecond day being twice drawne vp by the Pulley, he ſeemed very feeble; vpon this they let him downe to the ground, and looſned his cords, when inſtantly he dyed, not without ſtrong ſuſpition that he had poiſoned himſelfe, as appeared by the tokens in his body. So by the Sentence of Iuſtice hee was carried by the Hangman to the publike place of execution, and there buried.

A rumour was ſpred abroad by ſome falſe Calumniators, that this *Ruſca* was tortured

tured to death in prison, by the malice of those of the Religion: but worthy men of both the Religions that were then and there present, can witnesse the contrarie: because, during the two daies wherein he was tortured, he was not in all aboue one houre on the Torture: besides, his torture was most easie, but his death came by some other meanes, as hath beene declared.

The first day of *September*, *Iohn-Antonio Giouer da Calanca* was called in question, whose owne Letter, and others, with their Processe and witnesses doe testifie, that he had plotted to bring a warre vpō his Countrey, and to this end had sought to raise Forces in forraine States.

Iohn-Battista Zambra, of whom we haue formerly made mention, hath confessed, that *Giouer* had not onely conueyed his Letters and directions to *Millan*, but also that hauing written to him to be ready at the seruice of the house of *Millan*, and to hinder the Leauy of the Three Confederations against the building of Fort *Fuentes*, the said *Giouer* had returned him this answere; That he would aduance the busi-

nesse

nesse as much as hee could.

He hath by his Letters and Spies discouered the secret Counsailes of the Three Confederations Generall to forraine Princes, making offer to procure a good issue to their affaires, rather then to those of his owne Countrey. By his counsaile the passage of *Millan* was shut vp, so was it by vs to them of that State: yet he by his Office suffered many horses and other things to passe from this State thither, and hath craftily wrought that the Salt and Graine of that State might be kept from hence: hauing also secretly distributed money here, to corrupt others against the Priuiledges of our higher Powers.

He hath, contrarie to the Liberty of our Religion and publique Peace, stirred vp certaine Comminalties of the Three Confederations Generall, one against another by lies and false reports: and namely, he counsailed and helped to burne the Seates of the Protestants in the Church of *Masoch*, their Bels to bury vnder ground, and driue out the Ministers; wherein himselfe was a principall Actor, and for which worthy seruice he

was

was Knighted by the Pope, to whom hee tooke his Oath, contrary to the Allegeance he owes to his owne Countrey.

Hee published a counterfeit Proclamation at *Morbegno,* in the name of the Three Confederations Generall, That those who goe to *Venice,*should not onely be denied entertainment and lodging, but also hee that should kill any of them,should be free from all danger of punishment or Fine. Many other notorious outrages he hath committed, not needfull here to be related. Being therefore two seuerall times summoned to the Court of Iustice, and not appearing,he was banished, and had like Sentence of condemnation with that of Captaine *Rodulphus Planta.*

The same day Processe was framed by due course of Iustice against *Lucio di Monte,* chiefe Iudge of the *Grison* Confederation, for that it was euidently prooued by his owne Letters, and others,and by diuers witnesses, that he made his way to that Office by the money of forreine Princes, assisting them and their affaires in matter of State, with all his power ; receiuing at one time two hundred Doubles of *Spaine* from a Secretarie to a forreine Prince, and from another Prince three hundred gold Crownes for the like seruice. Hee hath likewise receiued much money from a certaine Embassadour of a forraine Prince, and disbursed seuen hundred Crownes for obtaining the Office of *Lantama*, or chiefe Iustice of *Lugniz* with corruption and presents: and yet (to the terrour of all men) tooke his corporall Oath, that he entertained no secret practice with any forraine State.

While hee was in his office of supreme Iudge and *Lantama*, he countenanced and furthered the seditious tumult of 1617. whereby many good men were persecuted, the Confederation of *Cadè* brought into great expenses, and the Three Confederations Generall into extreme danger. He hath further threatened when State matters were in handling, that vnlesse they succeeded as he would haue them, he would cause to be made such a hauock and spoile among them, as it should reach to their destruction and losse of life. He shewed his readinesse to receiue 50000. Crownes, for solliciting

the

the vniust Articles of the League with *Millan,* and working vs to a consent thereunto: wherein notwithstanding, the rest of his Complices would not giue their consent,for feare, if the League should goe forward, he would keepe all the money to himselfe. Moreouer, hee hath held strict practices with forrenners,to the great preiudice of our State, and hath dared to bragge that he had seuenteene of our Comminalties within the League of *Cade,*at his command, and in the rest of our Confederations he was growne so powerfull and strong, as he nothing esteemed the contrarie partie : whereby hee became so insolent, as he would force them to his ends by open violence,or else threaten to kill them like Calues. Lastly, he hath demanded Armes, with succours of forraine States against his owne Countrey.

Hereof being conscious, and of many other villanies, he is fled the Countrey and Liberties thereof : and being summoned by the Court of Iustice, and not making apparance, he was banished, and receiued like Sentence of condemnation with *Pompeius Planta.*

Some few daies after, *Iohn* Biſhop of *Coira* was accuſed, who eleuen yeeres ſince had beene baniſhed by order of Law, and impartiall iudgement of both the Religions of the Three Confederations Generall, for many foule crimes, and other tranſgreſſions againſt his Countrey: namely, for aduiſing and aſſiſting that the Three Confederations Generall might not keepe their Oath and couenant (which they ought) with other Princes and forrain States their Colleagues: and for receiuing and disburſing diuers ſummes of money, that wee might oppoſe the Lords of *Switzerland* our faithfull Neighbours and Confederates. Likewiſe, he put his Biſhopricke vnder the Protection of thoſe that were our profeſſed and ſworne enemies, and knowing himſelfe guilty of this perfidie, he laboured (in caſe his villanies ſhould come to light) to hold the Office of a Legate in the Countries of Germanie.

Not long after, contrarie to the Proclamation of the Three Confederations for his baniſhment, he being confederate with the diſloyall and traiterous men of our

Coun-

Countrey, who had then the power of the Supreme Magistrate in their owne hands, and returning to his Bishopricke at *Coira*, whither he was brought by *Rodulphus Planta*, chiefe head of the Treason against his Countrey, he hath here continued in his former practices, and persisted in his pernicious complottings against the State. Hee hath robbed our House neere *Fustemburgh* in his Diocesse, and hath placed therein a perfidious person, and one banished our State.

Hee hath contrarie to Law taken away the Hæreditarie Lands belonging to his Bishoprick, from those that possessed them by descent, but were not of his Episcopall faction, and giuen them to others of his owne partie. He hath aliened and conueied away diuers Lands from his Church, without the consent or knowledge of the League of *Cade*, which is Visiter and Protector of that Bishoprick; and hath employed wicked, perfidious, and temerarious persons, in his seruice, and against the State. He hath preached in Villages of matters of State, contrarie to his Oath, and the dignitie of his calling. He hath taken bribes in differences and ſuites in Law betweene party and party, concerning the Limits and boundaries of our Countrey, euer aſſiſting that ſide which oppoſed vs. He ſtileth his confederates that are of the reformed Religion, by the name of Heretiques, when he mentioneth them to forraine Princes, contrarie to the peace of our Religion and Countrey. He hath denied them buriall in that part of his Iuriſdiction which is out of our Countrey, ſo as they are forced to bring the corps hither to haue Chriſtian buriall: beſides many other Partialities. And hauing had notice that his actions were made knowne to the Comminalties and Councellors, he retyred himſelfe laſt yeere out of our Iuriſdiction: and being lawfully ſummoned to the Court, he failed to appeare. Herevpon the honourable Court of Iuſtice proceeded againſt him the 15. of *September* this preſent yeere, and vpon ſufficient examination of his own hand-writing, and others, diuers witneſſes being produced and heard, and all the premiſſes cleerely prooued, beſides many other; the Court hath decreed to adde new vigour to the former

mer

mer Proclamation of his banishment for life; confiscating all his own proper goods, and reseruing those of the Bishoprick: and hath further commanded the League of *Cadè*, and the Deane and Chapter of that Cathedrall Church, to proceed as speedily as conueniently they may, to the election of a new Bishop: straightly charging and forbidding all men to harbour him in the Countrey, and being taken there, to haue his head cut off.

Processe was likewise framed against many others, whose seuerall crimes & offences for breuities sake we omit. But besides the former, wee finde other wicked men so much corrupted and bribed with Presents and Donatiues from the Ministers of the French King, as they haue not onely promised to obserue the League, (in which case no bribes were needfull, euery man being resolued to keepe his Oath and beare himselfe as became his honour and reputation) but also to apply themselues in all things to the good will and pleasure of those publike Ministers: and accordingly, some seruants of his said Maiesty haue thrust

thrust themselues into businesses not comprized in the Articles, promising not to giue passage through our Countreys, (as if they were their owne) and not to giue their consent that we should enter League with any other.

These very men, vpon acknowledgement of great Donatiues and expectation of greater summes promised, haue likewise made themselues Vassals and humble Seruants to the Catholique Kings Embassadour in *Switzerland*, he hoping by this meanes to obtaine his demand in our Countrey ; namely, that the King his Master may be absolute Lord of all our passages. And yet these selfe-same men haue taken money of the *Venetians*, to further their demand of some Troupes of ours, or else to haue free passage for those they should leauy from other places ; or at least if any should fauour their affaire, to be silent, and heare and see nothing. By which meanes, drawing to themselues the treasures of other Princes, and impudently coozening both the one side and other, they haue brought our common Countrey into discredit and dis-

diſ-reputation : hence it is, that many of them who had but a ſmall patrimony left them by their Anceſtors, come now to liue ſplendidly, and grow infinitely rich.

Some of theſe men haue beene baniſhed their Countrey, and had they beene taken, they had beene ſentenced to be hanged and beheaded : ſome haue forfeited their eſtates, honours, and Armes ; others put out of our Councels; others haue loſt their money and goods; and many haue beene accuſed that haue cleered themſelues ; who not beeing conuicted of any crime, either by their own writing, confeſſion, or teſtimonie of honeſt and Legall men, they haue beene diſcharged without paying one penny of mulct, or Fees of the Court whatſoeuer.

So that in concluſion, whoſoeuer vvill take knowledge of our manner of proceeding, ſhall euidently ſee, that we haue beene forced thereunto by vrgent neceſſity. Firſt, that God the Lord of Hoſts might be glorified, who hath planted vs in this Eccleſiaſticall and Ciuill Liberty; and ſecondly, that our common Countrey might be preſerued by Iuſtice, to the extermination and baniſhment of all Treasons, the punishment of all notorious offences, the aduancement of true vertue and loyall honesty, the reformation of euill abuses, and restauration of our ancient Liberty, for the sincere and reall propagation thereof to our Posteritie.

And these are the true causes and reasons why we are falsely slandered and calumniated by our perfidious Countreymen and other malicious persons, blaming vs to other Princes and forraine States, as if this our Assembly and Iudiciall proceeding had been onely appointed for priuate factions, wicked emulations, hatred against the Romane Catholique Religion, and despight of our Confederates & ancient friends, to change them for new, & colleague our selues with them. But we are in good hope, that they who shall heare such persons talke, against whom we haue sent out our Processe and Proclamation, will likewise remember, that they are the same men who haue so falsely and so often deceiued forraine Princes and States our neighbours, receiuing great summes of money from them, and in word promising much in diuers places, but in effect perfor-

ming

ming nothing. And as they haue vainely ſought to excuſe their falſhood againſt their accuſers, ſo no doubt they will not be aſhamed with falſe machinations and pretences to palliate and cloke their malice.

If theſe ſo powerfull men haue beene faithfull Miniſters in the gouernment of our Countrey, and haue carried themſelues with ſuch integritie and ſinceritie towards all men, why doe other Princes and States complaine of our ill gouernment, and of our dayly changing our Councels, whereof theſe men haue beene the onely occaſion? Why doe they conteſt with Barons and Earles in all manner of riches and magnificence, and yet leaue the Countrey empty of all prouiſion? Can a Prince or forraine State complaine of any mans perfidie, and not of theſe, with whom he hath had ſo ſtrict intelligence, who promiſed them much, yet neither did nor could doe any thing? Who can charge vs to haue perſecuted any one Family or Comminaltie through faction or emulation, ſince it plainely appeareth, that the perſons executed were of diuers Families and Commi-

 nalties?

nalties? who will imagine they were falſely ſlandered of diuers things, when the Articles whereof they ſtood accuſed, appeared to be plainely prooued by their own handwritings, and thoſe of their Complices? Who will beleeue that their faults are aggrauated, and they condemned not being guilty, when their owne writings, actions, and confeſſions do plainely giue euidence, that the bloudy Fort *Fuentes* was built by their counſaile, aſſiſtance, and contribution? who alſo pronounced them enemies that hindred the worke, and bewrayed the ſecret deliberations of our Countrey, which were ſo honeſt, ſincere, and to no man preiudiciall: preſcribing vs the way how to carry our ſelues in that buſineſſe, that through feare we might become baſe and puſillanimous; to which ſeruice they were drawne by money, like vile and mercenary perſons.

But they ſay we haue a particular Faction by which they are perſecuted. This which they call Faction, is that which deſireth to aduance, preſerue, and defend the Honour and Word of God, conſiſting of all the reall

and

and true Subiects of our Countrey of both Religions. This is the Faction, that desireth to keepe the Liberties of our Countrey, according to our ancient lawes and ordinances. This is the Faction, that desireth to maintaine their Faith, Honour, and Oath, with all their Confederates. This is the Faction, that now for many yeeres hath promised to receiue no Pension of forraine Princes for matters of State, and that neuer made promise of any thing that it hath not faithfully performed; and for long time hath with much patience and more griefe endured such wicked persons. These are the children and posteritie of those that haue freed themselues from Tyrants, and will no longer acknowledge their Successors as Superiours, but as neighbours; and these are they that sustaine & support themselues by their integritie; they hate all Arrogancy and Ambition; they desire not to thrust their fingers into Princes Treasures, but serue them faithfully and honestly for their Pay in all their occasions, when they are required, and who venture their liues and goods with all readinesse and obedience for the defence of Iustice, and ſuppreſ-ſion of violence. In concluſion, this is the Faction that neuer could, can, or will indure ſo many groſſe abuſes and ſeditious practi-ces againſt our Countrey.

These perfidious perſons muſt needs haue a feeling (if not in themſelues, yet by others) that all men haue the glory of God, and the truth of their owne Religion in tender re-commendation, and that euery one thinkes in his owne conſcience, it is a deadly ſinne not to defend it, and reſiſt the Perſecuters thereof: and yet theſe men ſhame not to giue out, and publiſh to the world, that our end is nothing elſe but to perſecute the Ca-tholique Romane Religion, and to driue it out of our Countrey.

Had the Romane Catholiques alone made this complaint, perchance ſome might haue beleeued them; but why then do they of the reformed Religion complaine, who (as they ſay) are not moleſted? Why then doe both the Religions with hand and heart vnite themſelues in theſe proceedings for defence of their Countrey, and maintenance of their ancient liberties? Why doe both

Reli-

Religions ſit together in Court of Iuſtice at this preſent, with equity and indifferency to puniſh offenders both Reformed and Romane? But theſe bad men kept long ſecret in their boſomes this their calumniation and ſlander, till now the water of the Fountaines runnes ſo cleere, as they can no longer by troubling it, diſturbe the peace of our Countrey: and therefore now vpon diſcouery of their perfidious and falſe hearts, they vſe this falſe pretext of Religion, to withdraw our Subiects from their Countries ſeruice, and to draw our neighbour Princes and others, not to further with ſuch zeale as they ought, the good ſucceſſe of theſe our proceedings. Let them giue leaue to the honeſt and good men of our Countrey who are ſtill among vs, to complaine in this particular of Religion, of whom we firmely beleeue that no one man of either Profeſſion will euer open his lips, becauſe we haue neuer ſuffered in all our proceedings, that the leaſt violence ſhould be vſed to the one, or the other.

They ſay we haue put to death the Archprieſt of *Sondrio*: To this we anſwere, It is true,

true, and hee had but iustice; yet haue wee not taken away the Benefice, but haue giuen order for another to be chosen in his place,to discharge that Office: Nor did we proceed against him, for that he was a Priest, but for his bloudy deeds,his wicked counsailes, and Treasons. In like manner the Bishop of *Coira* stands out-lawed and banished, but his Bishoprick is not abolished; and another in his stead is to haue the possession. Besides, there haue beene mo of the reformed Religion punished, then of Catholiques.

It seemes in these our daies, that Religion is vsed as a cloke and pretext for vvicked and nefarious actions, and it is the ordinarie custome of those men to serue their turnes with such excuses,who in their life and conuersation neuer shewed any acknowledgement of Religion at all: nor haue any pretence of truth, to approoue the innocencie and integritie of their actions.

We are likewise charged to haue despised and set at nought the Maiesties of other Monarches in a barbarous manner,by renouncing our Faith giuen them, and quitting our friend-

friendſhip and Allyance with them. But we knowing well, that to deſpiſe and calumniate the ſaid Maieſties is vtterly againſt the Chriſtian Faith ; wee doe therefore hold them in all reuerent eſteeme and obſeruation, and thinke our ſelues much honoured, if we enioy their good fauour and friendſhip : yet neither may nor can wee by any meanes approoue the vndiſcreet and inconuenient actions of ſome of their Seruants : we hold them for our Confederates, but we are not tied to them in any ſpeciall duties, or ſeruices not comprized in their Commiſſion, nor ſpecified in the Articles of League with vs.

Who can truely ſay, or charge any Deliberation or Councell of ours, to haue renounced or broken any League or intelligence we had with others ?

We both in generall and in particular are readie, to maintaine towards all men our Faith, Credit, Honour, Oath, and good correſpondencie, and neighbourhood. And albeit ſome Embaſſadours by their vndiſcreet carriages haue prouoked vs to iuſt diſpleaſure, yet haue wee no purpoſe to diminish any one point in our interchange-able Leagues with others, or to molest and trouble them any way, onely wee could wish, that those Ministers of State were prescribed a better course how to carry themselues, or else that their Masters would call them home, and send others in their place.

If our People were so temerarious and head-strong as these calumniators would make the world beleeue; we, adhering to them as Authours of all lewdnesse, should euery yeere haue made Leagues and broken them, like these our slanderers, who haue wrought their vttermost among vs to renounce and quit all our true and reall Confederations, which, by the constancie and faithfulnesse of our People, and some of our Heads and Councellours, wee still maintaine in their force and inuiolable: and if any fault hath beene made, or failing in duties whereto wee were obliged by Article, the blame is to be laid vpon those perfidious Patriots, who like Merchants suffered themselues to be wonne with money, by their false shadowes and pretences of danger, to turne our *Common People* from the right way, who hold among vs the supreme Authoritie.

By all which things aforesaid, wee hope that euery man (especially such as know what true libertie is, and wherein it consisteth) shall haue occasion for the time to come, to iudge more modestly of our actions, without giuing eare to false pretences, or fauouring the said perfidious Countreymen of ours, by vs iustly banished; but shall banish them likewise out of their limits, as persons most wicked, and deseruing any kinde of punishment.

GOD, who changeth Kingdomes, setteth vp and pulleth downe Kings, enlargeth Dominions, and raiseth the Humble, keepe in his gracious fauour and protection all States and Common-wealths, defend them from Warre and Treason, from suspicions and iealousies; confounding all perfidious practices by his mightie Power, and preseruing all good Gouernments by his infinite Mercy. *Amen.*

AND to the intent that the world may know, how much these mercenary men of ours tooke vpon them, by propounding and procuring to sell our Libertie, and Treasury to Princes and forraine States: we haue set downe word by word, the Articles of the League betweene his Maiesty of Spaine, *and our Countries, to which League they perswaded our Commons in the yeere* 1617.

Articles drawne and to bee agreed vpon *the* 9. *of March* 1617. *by the most Illustrious* Don Alfonso Casale, *Councellor and Embassadour for the Catholique Maiestie in* Switzerland; *in the name and behalfe of the most Illustrious Prince* Don Pietro di Toledo, *Gouernour of the State of* Millan, *on the one party: and the Lords the Heads, and Deputies of the Three high Confederations Generall of* Grisons *on th' other partie: with the good liking and approbation of his Maiestie, and of the said Three Confederations Generall.*

WHereas there hath euer beene a good, sincere, and faithfull amitie, neighbourhood,

hood, and correſpondencie betweene the Duke of Millan, *and the Three Confederations Generall; the which, euer ſince the High and Mighty Kings of* Spaine *haue beene Lords of that State, hath beene continued by their Maieſties: therefore both the parties, vpon due conſideration of the happineſſe, profit and ſecuritie, which ariſeth from the good affection, ſinceritie, and louing intelligence betweene them; and to the intent that all cauſe of iealouſie and diffidence might bee remooued, which hath or might heretofore happen betweene the Maieſtie of* Philip *the third, and the ſaid Three Confederations Generall; and that a perpetuall good intelligence, faithfull neighbourhood, and a reall and mutuall vnion might be eſtabliſhed betweene them: they haue to the honour and glory of* GOD, *and to the publique good and ſafety, ioyntly reſolued to conclude this preſent Capitulation, Treatie, and Vnion, to ſtand in the full force and vertue of a continuall and hereditary League.*

And therefore the moſt Illuſtrious Prince and Lord, Don Pietro di Toledo *Generall of* Millan, *in the name and behalfe of his Maieſtie, and his ſucceſſors Dukes of* Millan *on th' one party, and the High and Noble Lords the Presidents, Councellors, and Comminalties of the Three Confederations Generall on the other partie, doe promise, that betweene his Maiestie as Duke of* Millan, *together with the Subiects of the said Duchy, and the Three Confederations Generall, with all their Subiects in* Valtelina, Bombio, *and the County of* Chiauenna, *shall be a true, sincere, and perpetuall amitie, correspondencie, neighbourhood, and union; so as neither partie shall suffer themselues to be imployed upon any seruice or occasion, to the preiudice and hurt of the other; nor shall suffer that through their Countreys or their Subiects, any passage, counsaile, or aide shall bee giuen directly or indirectly, which may secretly or openly damnifie either party, but that they shall oppose and resist them with all possible diligence and power. And when either of the parties shall know or understand any secret practice or attempt, whereby may bee engaged the preiudice and hurt of the other; that then they shall without delay giue notice thereof, and procure with all diligence and faithfulnesse to diuert the same.*

And

And because his Excellencie vnderstandeth, that the Three Confederations Generall would willingly that the Fort built in the yeere 1603. *vpon the Confines of* Valtelina *were demolished, as a pawne and pledge that they were againe restored into the good fauour and assured confidence of his Maiestie; hee promiseth, in testimonie of his Maiesties good affection to the Three Confederations Generall, That, so soone as this said Capitulation shall be concluded, sworne, and signed by both the parties, forthwith the Fort and Sconce belonging to it, shall effectually and really be demolished: and that the said Fort shall neuer be re-built, so long as the Contents of this Capitulation be faithfully and inuiolably kept, and no second cause bee giuen his Maiestie of diffidence and doubt of them, as was in the yeere* 1603. *And forasmuch as the said Lords Presidents, Councellors, and Comminalties of the Three Confederations Generall, doe know that the reason of that diffidence and doubt, which caused the building of the Fort was, in regard of the League and passage granted to the State of* Venice *the yeere before; they therefore promise for themselues and their Successors,*

cessors, neuer to renew the said League or passage, nor to giue their consent thereunto, so long as this Capitulation shall continue.

That commerce, negotiation, and passage shall bee free through both their Countries, and for all their Subiects without exception of persons, of what qualitie and condition so euer: but with this prouiso, that in their Letters of credence there be no scandall, nor bring in with them prohibited bookes, and that in time of Pestilence or Plague, the ancient customes be obserued. And concerning the Toll of Cattle or other commodities, which shall be brought into the State of Millan, *they shall enioy the like liberties with those already granted to such Swisse Cantons as are confederate with his Maiestie.*

And in case it so happen that his Maiestie shall haue neede of the Souldiers of this Countrey to defend his Duchy of Millan, *he shall haue a Leauy granted him by the Three Confederations Generall, of foure thousand men at the most, and two thousand at the least, (but all to be voluntaries;) reseruing notwithstanding a power in the Three Confederations Generall, to grant a greater number at*

their

their pleasure : The choise of the Collonell and Captaines to bee made by his Maiesties Embassadour : who hauing made the said Leauie, hee shall agree with the Collonell and Captaines chosen, for their Armes and Pay.

And in case his Maiestie would cause to passe into his Duchie of Millan, *through the Countrey of the Three Confederations Generall, or of their Subiects, any number of forraine Souldiours, for the preseruation and defence of his Duchy or other his States, free passage shall bee granted to his Captaines and Officers, so as their Troopes consist of no more then two hundred men, and that they bee alwaies distant one dayes iourney the one from the other. Euery Troope also shall haue his Captaine or Leader, and also one Commissary appointed by the Three Confederations Generall, at the charge of his Maiestie, to see that good order and discipline be kept, for the auoiding of all inconueniences; which Souldiours shall pay for their victuals, and other customes, and shall beare themselues quietly & peaceably throughout the Countrey.*

They ſhall beare no other Armes but Sword and Dagger, if they bee on foote; and they on horſebacke, nothing but their Piſtols: and in caſe it ſhall appeare by proofe, that theſe Souldiours haue damnified the Countries of the Three Confederations Generall, that then his Maieſtie ſhall be bound to make reſtitution.

On th' other ſide, if it ſhould ſo happen that the Three Confederations Generall were ſet vpon in hoſtile manner by any Prince, Potentate, or free State, that then his Maieſtie ſhall be bound vpon euery their demand, to ſend to their ſuccours two thouſand foot, and two hundred horſe, vpon his owne expence till the warre bee ended: and in caſe the Three Confederations Generall ſhould ſtand in neede of greater ſuccours, his Maieſtie ſhall be bound to ſend them forthwith: But if the Three Confederations Generall ſhall finde it more for their aduantage, or like it better to haue money then Souldiours; that then his Maieſtie ſhall truely pay them ten thouſand Crownes a moneth, ſo long as their warre laſteth, and ſhall lend them ſixe Peeces of Artillerie and Munition thereunto belonging, as

farre

farre as the vttermost bounds of the Countie of Chiauenna, *with condition that the warre being done, the Artillerie bee restored.* *It shall bee lawfull for the Three Confederations Generall and their Subiects, to buy at the Faire of* Como *and* Palanza *in the Duchy of* Millan, *all sorts of Graine for euery mans vse and necessitie, with like freedome as those Swisse-Cantons doe, which are in League with his Maiestie.*

His Maiestie as Duke of Millan, *according to his wonted Princely Liberalitie, and to testifie his gracious fauour to the Three Confederations Generall, promiseth to pay into the Exchequer of each Confederation Generall yeerely, vpon* S^t^. Iohn Baptists *day, three thousand Florens, worth three shillings nine pence Sterling a-piece: This paiment to beginne the first* Saint Iohn Baptists *day after the Sealing and Swearing of this Vnion.*

And when any difference or dispute shall arise betweene his Maiestie and the Three Confederations Generall, two Arbiters shall be chosen of either party, who shall meet at Chiauenna *or* Lorico, *as the one or other partie shall be Plaintiffe or Defendant; and these differences betweene them in two moneths to bee cleerely determined and decided. And in case any difference arise betweene priuate persons of both the States, that then the Plaintiffe shall call the Defendant before his Magistrate and Iudge: but in case they cannot here be agreed, and their difference compounded, that then each of the Parties shall haue choise of one able man well experienced in causes of Iustice, out of the Aduersaries Countrey: and then to cast Lots which of these two shal determine the difference.*

That this present Capitulation shall bee no way preiudiciall to the League and Letter- Riuersall, made and giuen by the Three Confederations Generall with the Crowne of France: but that, that League and Letter shall still remaine in their force, and their owne proper words.*

That this present Capitulation shall bee perpetuall and hereditarie; his Maiestie reseruing on his part the holy Sea of Rome, *the Sacred Romane Empire, the High and Mighty House of* Austria, *his League with the Catholique-Cantons of* Switzerland, *and all other his ancient Leagues and Treaties. And*

on

*on the other part, the Three Confederations Generall reseruing the Sacred Romane Empire, their League and Letter-*Riuersall with the Crowne of* France, *their perpetuall Vnion with the High and Mighty House of* Austria, *their Confederation with the Cantons of* Switzerland, *and all other their ancient Leagues which haue beene formerly inuiolably and effectually kept and obserued.*

FINIS.